Mexican

ART & CULTURE

Elizabeth Lewis

Raintree

www.raintreepublishers.co.uk
Visit our website to find out more information about **Raintree** books.
To order:
 Phone 44 (0)1865 888113
 Send a fax to 44 (0)1865 314091
 Visit the Raintree bookshop at **www.raintreepublishers.co.uk** to browse
our catalogue and order online.

First published in Great Britain by Raintree, Halley Court, Jordan Hill, Oxford OX2 8EJ,
part of Harcourt Education.
Raintree is a registered trademark of Harcourt Education Ltd.

© Harcourt Education Ltd 2004
The moral right of the proprietor has been asserted.

Editorial: Nancy Dickmann and Louise Galpine
Design: Ron Kamen and Paul Davies and Associates
Illustrations:
Picture Research: Peter Morris and Maria Joannou
Production: Séverine Ribierre

Originated by Dot Gradations
Printed and bound in China by South China Printing Company

ISBN 1 844 21045 6 (hardback)   ISBN 1 844 21050 2 (paperback)
07 06 05 04 03   08 07 06 05 04
10 9 8 7 6 5 4 3 2 1   10 9 8 7 6 5 4 3 2 1

British Library Cataloguing in Publication Data
Lewis, Elizabeth
     World Art and Culture: Mexican
     709.7'2
A full catalogue record for this book is available from the British Library.

The publishers would like to thank the following for permission to reproduce photographs: AKG pp. **30**,
39; Alamy p. **48**; Alamy pp. **6** (Angel Terry), **13** (Ethel Davies/ Imagestate), **21** (Sue Clark), **40** (Anna
Gordon/Andes Press Agency); Andes Press Agency p. **19** (Carlos Reyes-Manzo); Art Archive p. **31**; Art
Archive pp. **43** (Bibliotheque de l'Assemblee Nationale Paris/ Mireille Vautier), **38** (National History
Museum Mexico City/ Dagli Orti); Corbis pp. **33** (Catherine Karnow), **24** (Charles and Josine Lenars), **9**
(Charles Lenars), **37** (Archivo Icongrafico), **49** (Sygma/ Servin Humberto), **42**, **51** (Danny Lehman), **27**
(Macduff Everton), **23** (Michael T. Sedam), **11** (Randy Faris), **29**, **32**, **46** (Sergio Dorantes), **26** (David
Houser), **20** (Gerald French), **14**, **36** (Gianni Dagli Orti), **7**, **15** (Werner Forman); Panos pp. **17**, **18**, **25**; Panos
pp.**4** (Piers Benatap) **50** (Roderick Johnson), **34** (S.Molins); South American Pictures pp. **47**(Charlotte
Lipson), **45** (Chris Sharp), **44** (Tony Morrison).

Cover photograph of hanging fabrics, reproduced with permission of Punchstock/Brand X, and of jade
funerary mask, reproduced with permission of The Art Archive/National Anthropological Museum,
Mexico/Dagli Orti.

The publishers would like to thank Eleanor Wake and Amber Da for their assistance in the preparation of
this book.

Contents

Words printed in the text in bold, **like this**, are explained in the Glossary.

Introduction

Mexican art reflects the rich mixture of traditions and cultures found in Mexico. There are many different **indigenous** peoples in Mexico, who have their own languages and customs and who can trace their history back many hundreds of years to peoples such as the Aztecs, Maya and Toltecs. Today, these traditional groups live alongside people whose ancestors came originally from Europe – particularly from Spain – and there are many **mestizos** (people whose family is a mix of both Indian, Mexican and European people). But they are all Mexicans and part of North America, and the mix of native, European and American traditions has formed a country where almost everyone creates art in some way – you can see it all around you.

Three important eras

You can divide Mexican history into three main different periods. Each one produced its own type of art which was very different to the others. **Pre-Hispanic** describes the period between 1200 BCE and 1519. It includes the civilizations of the Olmecs, Maya, Teotihuacán, the Toltecs and Aztecs. Each of these groups produced their own distinctive styles of art. In 1519 Hernán Cortés arrived from Spain and conquered the Aztecs. This is when the **Post-Conquest** period began – much of the art produced during this time was influenced by Spain. In 1821 Mexico won its independence from Spain and the art since this time reflects the country's renewed sense of pride in a culture and history that was distinct and native to Mexico.

Mexico is a very diverse country made up of many different regions, each producing its own particular type of art.

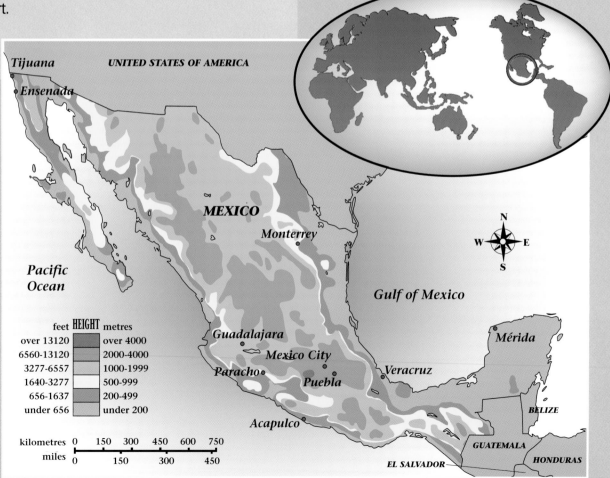

UNITED STATES OF AMERICA

Tijuana

Ensenada

MEXICO

Monterrey

Pacific
Ocean

Gulf of Mexico

N
W   E
S

feet HEIGHT metres	
over 13120	over 4000
6560-13120	2000-4000
3277-6557	1000-1999
1640-3277	500-999
656-1637	200-499
under 656	under 200

Guadalajara

Mexico City

Paracho

Puebla

Veracruz

Mérida

BELIZE

Acapulco

GUATEMALA

EL SALVADOR

HONDURAS

kilometres 0   150   300   450   600   750
miles   0   150   300   450

4

Craftspeople often wear traditional Mexican clothes, particularly in the more rural areas of Mexico.

Many regions

Mexico is made up of many different regions, from deserts in the north to rainforest in the south. In each of these regions live groups of people, each with their own way of life, and often with their own language – there are currently around 50 Native American languages being spoken in Mexico. From remote mountainous areas to big cities like Mexico City, Mexican life involves a mix of the traditional – which often varies from region to region – and the modern.

North and south

It is important to remember that Mexico is just across the border from the USA – in fact, California, Texas and Florida were all at one time part of Mexico. Both countries influence each other. By contrast, to the south of Mexico lies Guatemala – a country of mountains and rainforest where the Mayan culture lives on.

Religion and ritual

Most Mexicans today are Catholic. A lot of the art that they make reflects their beliefs. Throughout the year, there are many religious festivals for which special pieces of art are made.

Mexico became a Catholic country when the Spanish conquered it. Until then, the people living there had worshipped spirits and different sorts of gods to do with things from nature, like the Sun, the Moon and the Earth. Their worship involved a lot of special **rituals** and the people made many artistic images of their gods, or of their rulers, whom they considered godlike.

A wide variety

The existence of so many different regions, languages, foods and cultures means that a huge variety of art is produced in Mexico, using all sorts of different materials. Most of these raw materials can be found near to where the art is being made.

An ancient culture

Much of the art that has been produced in Mexico was made hundreds of years ago. A great deal of this art has survived and gives us a lot of information about the people who created it.

The Olmecs are one of the oldest known civilizations in the Americas, flourishing between 1200 and 300 BCE. They were particularly good sculptors and carved enormous heads out of rock. One of their favourite subjects to carve was a *werejaguar*. This was a creature which mixed features from a human and a jaguar.

Teotihuacán was a city-state in the Valley of Mexico, and lies about 40 kilometres (25 miles) north-east of today's Mexico City. During the period from around 100 to 650 CE, it was one of the largest cities in the world and was a very powerful and influential cultural centre. Its people built incredible monuments such as the Pyramid of the Sun, which was more than 60 metres high, and the Pyramid of the Moon, which was slightly smaller.

The Mayan culture flourished from 300 CE to 900 CE in the area from the Yucatán **peninsula** in Mexico, to what is now Guatemala, Belize and Honduras. The Maya area in Mexico stretched between the modern states of Chiapas and Quintana Roo. The Maya are best known for the amazing cities they built – such as Palenque – with pyramids that had beautiful carvings and painted murals.

This head has been carved from a single block of **basalt** by the Olmecs. There are eighteen heads like this one around Mexico and they can be up to 3 metres tall and weigh up to thirty tonnes. The helmet is thought to signify royalty.

1200–300 BCE: Olmec civilization flourishes, beginning in the eastern coastal lowlands around the area we now know as Veracruz.

*c.*1150 BCE: The Olmecs carve enormous stone male heads.

300 BCE–900 CE: Mayan civilization occupies the area now known as Guatemala, Honduras and the Yucatán Peninsula.

The Toltecs had a very sophisticated culture – their name means 'master builders'. They existed between the 9th and 13th centuries CE, when they built many pyramid temples in an area called Tula. One of these is known as the Plumed Serpent and was dedicated to the god Quetzalcoatl.

The Aztecs were at their most powerful between the 14th and 16th centuries. They created an immense empire centred on the city of Tenochtitlán – the site of modern Mexico City. They fashioned beautiful art from gold in honour of one of the gods they worshipped – the Sun. Spanish soldiers conquered the Aztecs between 1519 and 1521.

The arrival of the Spanish

The Spaniard Hernán Cortés led an expedition to Mexico in 1519. He marched to Tenochtitlán, the Aztec capital, where he was welcomed by Montezuma, the Aztec emperor, who thought Cortés was a god and presented him with a beautiful feathered headdress. Cortés imprisoned Montezuma and conquered the Aztecs in 1521. The period in history that followed is called the Colonial period. The **Native Americans** were **exploited** and were treated almost as slaves under the Spanish. Many different social classes were created, depending on where you lived and whether your ancestors were Spanish or Native American. There was lots of rivalry between these classes and some were more powerful than others.

A terracotta statue of a Mayan noble wearing traditional ceremonial dress.

100–750 CE: The highly developed Teotihuacán civilization flourishes.

700 CE–1200 CE: Teotihuacán declines around 700 CE and the people move north to Tula around 10th century CE.

1325–1519: Aztec civilization. The nomadic Aztec tribe built the city of Tenochtitlán – now Mexico City.

An important change at this time was that Roman Catholicism became the national religion instead of the worship of native gods. Much of the art that was made at this time – both by the Native Americans and by the descendants of the Spanish colonists – was influenced by the Catholic religion.

Independence and revolution

In 1821 Mexico won its independence. One of the agreements of the independence treaty was that the Spanish and *criollos* – Mexicans of European descent – were granted equal rights. There then followed a long period of instability and a period of revolution from 1910 to 1920. A leading figure in the revolution was Emiliano Zapata, who fought for the rights of the rural population. He has become the subject of many legends and ballads in Mexico. The Revolution in Mexico was a very disruptive time, and many works of political art were produced, especially in the form of **murals** painted on the outsides of buildings.

Mexico today

Today, Mexico is a country of great contrasts. Many people have moved away from the countryside to the cities – and there is a big difference between living in a Mexican city and living in a remote village. Mexico City is one of the largest cities in the world. However, many Mexicans are very poor. Many Mexicans have gone to the USA to find work, and as a result, Mexican art has spread into American culture, just as American culture has spread to Mexico.

Diego Rivera was famous for painting very striking murals on the outside of public buildings. He wanted to make sure as many people as possible saw his work and understood his political message.

1492: Christopher Columbus 'discovers' the Americas. Native Americans already inhabited the land.

1521: Hernán Cortés conquers the Aztecs. He captures the emperor Montezuma and **razes** the city of Tenochtitlán to the ground. Mexico City was built out of the ruins.

1821: Mexico granted independence from Spain by the Treaty of Córdoba. The Roman Catholic Church becomes the national religion.

1836: Texas wins independence from Mexico.

1845: Texas becomes part of the United States.

1846–1848: War with the United States.

1910: The Mexican Revolution begins. New laws are introduced and land is returned to the Native Americans.

1929: The Revolutionary Party is formed and rules Mexico until 2000.

2000: The Revolutionary Party is defeated by Vicente Fox of the National Action Party (PAN).

Architecture

If you travel around Mexico you will see an enormous variety of architecture. Whenever a new group of people came to power or settled somewhere different, they would make their mark by building palaces or temples in their own particular style. These monuments were all built using tools made out of stone, and all the transporting of the heavy materials was done by hand – until the last century no form of lifting machinery was used at all. Nowadays, Mexican architecture is built using all sorts of materials such as glass and aluminium, and the designs are very sophisticated and renowned throughout the world.

In Mexico today, most families are quite large and couples usually have more than one or two children. Most people have migrated to the cities where they live in modern houses. However, a quarter of the population still live in rural villages, in simple houses, sometimes made of *adobe* (mud bricks which have been left to dry in the hot sun), wood or other natural materials. These houses are very similar to the houses that Mexicans lived in centuries ago.

The Pyramid of the Sun in Teotihuacán is nearly 70 metres high and is one of the largest pyramids in the world. When it was built in around 150 CE it would probably have had a flat roof with a temple dedicated to the Sun god.

Teotihuacán

Teotihuacán was one of the greatest ancient Mexican cities. By around 550 CE, it is thought to have had a population of 125,000 people. The biggest structures in Teotihuacán were the Pyramid of the Sun and the Pyramid of the Moon. The Pyramid of the Sun is one of the largest structures to be built in the **Western hemisphere**. It is made of layers of clay faced with stone and is about 61 metres (200 feet) high. A flight of stairs leads to the **summit**, where a temple to the sun god Uitzilopochtli was originally erected. The pyramid's site was chosen as it is on the **axis** of the Sun's passage during the summer **solstice**. The movement of the Sun, Moon and stars was important to the religion of ancient Mexican peoples. The walls of temples and some homes were decorated with colourful **frescos**.

 ## Stelae, ball courts and palaces

The Maya also built other important stone monuments. Stelae, built as monuments to their leaders, were upright slabs or pillars of stone usually bearing an inscription, a carved sculpture and the date they were built. Like some other Native Americans, the Maya built ball courts. These were areas in a temple where games were played during a ceremony or possibly just for fun. Palaces were built much lower than the pyramids and had lots of rooms, although it is not thought that anyone lived in them as they were very damp and uncomfortable. They were more likely to have been used for **ritual** purposes.

The Maya

The Maya built a great civilization in Central America during the Classic period (between 300 and 900 CE). They resided mainly in the south of Mexico, and the main centre of their culture was in present-day Guatemala. Mayan art and architecture, and particularly their temples, are the most distinctive hallmarks of their civilization. At Tikal, one of the most important Mayan cities, you can see the remains of the pyramids that the Maya built. These pyramids were used for religious ceremonies and had thatch-roofed temples or altars on the top, where priests performed sacrifices to the gods. Several of the pyramids were grouped around an open **plaza**. The pyramids were quite distinctive as they were built as a series of steps and had a steep stairway built in the middle of one or more of the sides. The steps were made from stone blocks that had been skilfully cut by hand. The foundations of the pyramids were usually made of earth and **rubble** and were bonded with cement. The interiors were painted with bright colours and the outsides were lavishly decorated with painted sculptures, carved **lintels** and stone mosaics. Another distinctive feature of Mayan architecture was the corbeled arch. This is an arch that is supported by two **brackets** (corbels) made out of stone, wood or bricks.

A developed culture

The Aztecs founded their city at Tenochtitlán, which is the site of modern-day Mexico City. They built the city on a group of small islands in Lake Texcoco, constructing a complicated grid system of streets and canals around a set of pyramids, religious temples and stunning palaces which could be seen for miles around. They also built an intricate series of **causeways** and bridges to connect the city to the mainland. Impressive **aqueducts** were also constructed, and canals were used to transport goods and people.

From the Aztecs to modern Mexico

The Aztecs built a very **sophisticated** and extensive empire between the 14th and 16th centuries. But in 1521 the Spanish explorer Hernán Cortés captured the city of Tenochtitlán and destroyed it. From the ruins he built what we now know as Mexico City. The National Palace, which we can still see today, was built on the same site as the palace of the Aztec emperor Montezuma.

The Spanish **conquistadors** had a great impact on buildings throughout Mexico. This style is called Spanish **colonial** architecture and one of its distinguishing features is the *Plateresque* style, which was particularly popular in the 16th century. It was a very ornamental style which gave the appearance that silver had been applied to the walls of the buildings.

Another influence on Mexican architecture is from Native Americans. Many Spanish colonial buildings are decorated with Native American **motifs**. However by the 19th and 20th centuries much of the new architecture in Mexico City resembled the **ornate** style of the French – many buildings were very grand with lots of detailed decoration.

Renaissance in architecture

Today, many of Mexico's cities have wonderful examples of stylish modern buildings. From 1945 onwards there has been a **renaissance** in Mexican architecture, which has attracted attention from around the world. Architects suddenly became more interested in designing fresh modern buildings rather than keeping alive the styles of the past.

However, new buildings such as the main library of the National Autonomous University of Mexico, built by Juan O'Gorman, incorporate superb **murals** with frescos and mosaics that are a reminder of the wall paintings of their ancient architectural predecessors. The designs are based on the pictures that can be found in early Central Mexican manuscripts. The University is a fantastic example of the new energy that modern architects are putting into their work. Felix Candela, a Spanish architect who settled in Mexico, created the sports stadium for the 1968 Olympic Games held in Mexico City. He also built several churches, which had very unusual concrete shell designs.

The old and new

Guadalajara, capital of the state of Jalisco, is a wonderful example of a city that combines both traditional and modern styles of architecture. On the city's cathedral there is a mural called *The Assumption of the Blessed Virgin*, by Bartolomé Esteban Murillo, which is a very well known piece of Spanish colonial art. However, sitting quite comfortably alongside the traditional styles of building are some very striking examples of **modernist** architecture.

Today in Mexico there are many dramatic examples of modern architecture, such as the Stock Exchange in Mexico City.

Carvings and sculpture

Unlike some other **artefacts**, carvings often survive relatively intact and they can give us important clues about how people lived at the time the carving was created.

Olmec heads

The Olmecs were the first people in Mexico to build and carve things out of stone. In roughly 1150 BCE they began to carve enormous male heads out of **basalt** near modern-day Veracruz. Some of the heads had helmets and measured up to 3.6 metres (12 feet) high. Why they were carved remains a mystery. As well as these giant sculptures, the Olmecs carved small statues out of jade, which can be seen in Villahermosa.

The Maya carved many figures out of stone, and also created **intricate** carvings in relief. This means that the figures stood out from the background they were carved from.

Jade carving

Jade is a hard, green **opaque** gemstone which varies in colour from dark green to almost white. The Olmec, Aztec and Mayan civilizations all carved beautiful ceremonial objects out of jade. Axes, knives, masks and large animal figures were carved in great detail, showing the incredible skill these early craftspeople had achieved. The Maya were particularly keen on the gemstone, valuing it even more highly than gold. Archaeologists have discovered jade carvings inside Mayan burial chambers. It was fashionable for people of high status to have their teeth **inlaid** with decorative jade fillings.

The ancient Mexican civilisations valued jade more highly than gold. They were very skilful carvers and made many beautiful objects to commemorate special occasions.

The Sunstone

The carvings on the Sunstone tell us what the Aztecs believed about how the world was created and how they measured time. The stone is carved from basalt and it is 91 centimetres (3 feet) thick, 3.6 metres (12 feet) in diameter and weighed 22 tonnes. It is thought that the stone was painted in vibrant colours of red, blue, yellow and white. One of the inner rings is divided into twenty sections – the number of days in each Aztec month. The centre of the stone depicts how the Aztecs believed the Earth was created. They thought the Earth had been created five times, each time lasting for a period known as a 'sun'. The face in the middle of the stone may represent the fifth sun. The Aztecs believed that the Sun needed to be fed, and sometimes human sacrifices were made to repay the Sun for creating life on Earth.

The Aztec Sunstone (1427) took 52 years to complete because it is thought to have been carved using stone tools. Placed on top of the main temple in Tenochtitlán, the capital of the Aztec empire, it was lost for 250 years because it was buried by the Spaniards.

◈ How were the carvings made?

The Aztecs used tools made from **obsidian**, which is a glass-like volcanic stone that is extremely hard and can be even sharper than steel. Obsidian also made very good weapons – axe heads, knives and spear points were all carved from this very hard material. It is still used today to make surgical instruments. The Aztecs would use their obsidian tools to sculpt and carve decorative patterns.

Pottery and ceramics

Modelling objects out of clay has been practised for thousands of years in Mexico. It is a very skilled art and potters in Mexico have always been much admired. Some of the techniques used by the Aztecs are still being used today, particularly in more rural areas. Modern potters gather their clay from the local area. They make a lot of their pots by hand or use a wooden wheel that is turned by the potter. Some Mexicans today store their grain and carry their water in large pottery jars just as the Aztecs once did. They also need to make pots to earn a living. Once a week, village potters set off before dawn for market, their pots wrapped in dry grasses and corn husks to protect them from breakage.

Historical records

Unlike paper, pottery does not decay and it can provide valuable clues about how people lived. Some pieces of pottery have been discovered with detailed scenes painted on them, which show people going about their everyday lives. Finding a piece of pottery like this is very exciting for an **archaeologist**, as it tells us the type of clothes people wore, the animals they kept, and the way they farmed the land. Pottery can also tell us how much one group of people communicated with another. If the pottery from two different areas is similar, then it is possible that these two groups may have met and exchanged ideas with each other.

The **Lancandón** people, who live in Najá, are descended from the Mayan people and their way of life has changed very little over centuries. Unlike a lot of **indigenous** groups in Mexico, they have not adopted Christianity and they make objects out of clay, which are offerings to their gods. All sorts of things are made out of pottery, from everyday objects like cups and plates, to more decorative items like incense burners, flutes, whistles and candlesticks.

 ## Firing the pots

After a pot is formed, it must be **fired** to harden the clay and make it watertight. Methods of **firing** the finished pot vary. In some areas, potters still place their pots in the ashes of an open fire as the Aztecs did, whereas other areas have adopted more modern methods and use an enclosed oven, or **kiln**. Traditionally, wood is used to keep the fire going, but more and more people are using **kerosene** instead.

 ## Pots in the afterlife

When Aztec potters were buried, it was traditional that some of their pots were buried with them. This tells us that the Aztecs believed in an **afterlife** as they were expecting to use their pots after they were dead.

Specially designed cooking utensils

Mexico is **renowned** for its traditional food. Maize (used to make **tortillas**), chilli, tomatoes and beans are all ingredients that have been present in the Mexican diet for centuries. Mexicans have designed special implements to cook their food and a lot of them were made from clay – a natural resource. They discovered that the secret behind different cooked food flavours was in the clay used to make the cooking utensils. Many of these utensils are still used to prepare food today and they give Mexican food a distinctive 'earthy' taste. The following utensils are all made from clay:

- *Cazuelas* are like casseroles and vary in depth, size, shape and decoration. They can be used as saucepans, mixing bowls, and baking and serving dishes.
- *Ollas* are pots which give food an authentic flavour when ingredients are blended together. Sauces simmer in the pots to speed up the blending process.
- *Jarros* are pitchers which traditionally have the owner's name painted on before they are glazed. They are often used for holding drinking water.

This pottery that has been given a green glaze is distinctly Mexican. All sorts of pottery objects – some practical, some just decorative – can be found throughout the country.

Methods and materials

The methods used to make clay pots vary from region to region. People in some areas are still using the same techniques as their ancestors; others are using more up-to-date methods. Instead of spinning the pot round by placing one dish on top of another upturned dish, which was the traditional way, a kick wheel operated with the foot means the pot can be spun round much faster and a more symmetrical pot can now be made.

Puebla is a city famous for its majolica earthenware, which is called *talavera*. The reason why there is so much pottery made in this region is because there is a great deal of clay in the earth around Puebla. As well as pots, Puebla is also famous for its brightly coloured *azulejos* – tiles which are used to decorate the outside of buildings and kitchens. Some of the potters still make *talavera* in the same way that the monks did in the 16th century – by treading the clay with their feet.

Not all pottery is made by hand. In some regions moulds are used. But this is not a new invention – the native peoples of Mexico used moulds to make their pots in **pre-Hispanic** times and the same method is used today. Flat sheets of clay are pressed into or over the mould, which has been sprinkled with ashes to prevent the clay sticking. Joins between the pieces of clay are smoothed over with the fingers or sometimes a maize cob.

Women in Oaxaca still make cooking pots by hand. The process takes a lot longer than using a mould, but each piece is individual and uniquely decorated.

◈ Oaxacan pottery

In some small villages in Oaxaca, the potters prefer the old methods. They hollow out the dark clay with their fists and smooth down the walls of the pot with a slither of broken pottery. A piece of wet leather is used to make the lip of the pot flare out. The women are in charge of decorating the pots. They scratch beautiful **motifs** on the sides using their nails, or sometimes they might make a more elaborate pattern by scratching a design with a twig or a feather.

Some original uses

As with a lot of other Mexican arts and crafts, particular celebrations have led to the making of certain pieces of pottery. Some potters in Jalisco spend all year making nativity scenes out of pottery to sell at Christmas time. These *nacimientos* depict a scene of the Christmas story and can take up the whole side of a room. Some potters specialize in gigantic **candelabra** known as 'trees of life', which are specially made for wedding couples. They are painted in the brightest of colours and most show scenes from the Bible, although some imaginative potters have included Batman in their trees!

In Metepec the *Arbol de la Vida* or tree of life has been made for more than 100 years. Originally the theme was the Garden of Eden but today all sorts of stories are told – they can even be autobiographical, telling the potter's or the customer's story. Generally the tree's stories are 'read' from bottom to top.

A relatively new development is the **glazing** of the pots. This gives the pots a shiny surface. You can often tell where a pot has come from by the colour of its glaze. Black and amber glazes are popular in many regions, and a green glaze is especially common in the state of Michoacán. Maiolica is a special type of glaze, made using tin. It has been made in Mexico since the time of the Spanish invasion, when it was used in the production of beautiful tiles to decorate the fronts of churches. Many different materials are used to make the glazes that decorate the pots – some are found locally, but others, such as tin, may be imported.

The colour of clay used also varies from region to region. In San Bartolo, Oaxaca, they produce a famous black clay called *barro negro*. Buff and brown ceramics tend to be found in the deserts, and red-brown colours called redware come from Michoacán and the areas around the mountains.

Textiles and clothes

Mexican clothes are very colourful and distinctive. It is easy to spot a piece of clothing that is typically Mexican. Many Mexicans, particularly those in rural areas, wear the same style of clothes their ancestors wore before the

Spanish arrived. It is their way of showing their origins. Typical items of clothing include the *huipil*, which is a woman's sleeveless tunic often with intricate embroidered flowers around the neck, the *quechquemitl*, a small triangular cape worn around the shoulders by women, and the *serape*, a blanket with an opening for the head, often worn by men to keep them warm when they are horseriding. Of course, not all Mexicans wear traditional dress – many dress in modern fashions and might only wear traditional clothing for special festivals.

Many Mexicans, particularly those who live in the more remote areas away from the big towns and cities wear brightly coloured traditional clothes very similar to those worn by their ancestors.

◈ A colourful country

The Mexicans are famous for their love of colour and have developed many ingenious techniques for dying their cloth. Traditionally, weavers use natural dyes to make their colours, although they are beginning to use **synthetic** dyes. Considerable skill and hard work is needed to achieve the right colours and the process can take several days. Fruits, flowers, leaves, barks and woods are used to dye the materials. Blackberries make a lovely purple, camomile leaves a greenish gold, and cochineal from the cochineal beetle, makes a distinctive red, although the beetle is now becoming quite rare.

Clothing and culture

For many Mexicans their clothes are important symbols – they are not just items to keep them warm or dry. Women and girls can be seen wearing wraparound skirts and a simple top called a *huipil*, and the men might wear palm hats and a tunic called a *colera*. Women often make clothes by hand for themselves and their families, using traditional techniques, which have remained the same for hundreds of years. They spend many hours carefully creating the cloth for their clothes. When they die, their **spindle** and needle and thread are buried with them. They believe they will need them to mend their clothes in the next world.

It is not just women who wear traditional clothes. Mexican men are also proud of their heritage and can be seen wearing very ornate outfits, particularly at celebrations. During festivals, when Mexican horsemen (*charros*) are displaying the skills of their horses, they wear elaborate belt buckles and silver ornaments on their large felt hats called *chapetas*. In many rural areas, the men sport traditional palm hats – very useful for protecting their heads from the sun. In some villages these hats are decorated with ribbons, feathers, beaded bands, colourful woollen pom-poms and even squirrel tails or beer bottle lids – anything that is bright, decorative and easily obtained is used.

Weaving on a backstrap loom is a very old Mexican tradition. It is usually done outdoors with one end of the loom fixed to a tree or pillar and the other tied around the weaver's body.

◈ Weaving technique

To weave cloth, it is necessary to combine the **warp** (vertical threads) and the **weft** (horizontal threads). In Mexico, this has been done for over 4000 years using something called a backstrap loom. This simple piece of apparatus is usually used outdoors, with one end tied around a tree and the leather back strap tied to the weaver, who controls the tension of the warp with her body. Blankets, shawls known as *rebozos*, shoulder-bags, sashes, skirts, rugs and tapestries are all made on the backstrap loom.

A very distinctive pattern

Each region in Mexico has its own particular style of dress and special weaving patterns. A Mexican could tell you where somebody comes from by looking at the design of their *serape* or their **poncho**. For example, a blanket with a rainbow pattern means the wearer comes from the Saltillo area of Mexico.

Many of today's textile arts are practised by women. They spend many hours weaving, spinning, or making embroidery, mostly by hand, to create distinctive pieces of clothing that are recognized all over the world.

Animal skins and plants

Techniques that the ancient people used to make clothes are still practised – crafts like tie-dying, tapestry, quilting and weaving are all very popular.

The ancient people made their clothes from materials that they could find around them. There are ancient murals which show men wearing tunics and short cloaks made from jaguar skins. Some of them are wearing very elaborate headdresses made from colourful feathers, which make them look like wild animals and gods – they wanted to look as important and frightening as possible. They also used to wear headdresses made from husks of maize, or corn on the cob, a crop grown all over Mexico.

Only the noblemen of the ancient civilizations were allowed to wear cotton, as it was very expensive. The lower classes had to wear material that was less comfortable. The Aztecs used to make some of their cloth from fibrous plants. One type, now called *henequen* was made from the maguey plant. They also used the bark of wild fig and other trees to get fibres which they could then weave into cloth.

Embroidery

The art of embroidery increased in popularity after the Spanish arrived. Today these skills are handed down from mother to daughter. The traditional designs are recorded on samplers – pieces of cloth that have been framed with all the different stitches sewn onto them. Mothers will use these samplers to teach their children the stitches – and there are many to learn. All the different stitches are used to personalize either a home-woven piece of cloth or a piece of material that has been bought in a shop. Satin-stitch is one of the most popular stitches. The stitches are made very close to each other, making sure there is no material in between – this creates the effect of a piece of satin. Animals, birds and flowers created using this stitch decorate *huipiles*, skirts and blouses.

The Huichol people, who live in a remote mountainous area of Mexico, are best known for their colourful yarn pictures. The embroideries contain many religious symbols such as the Dog Woman, whom they believed was the first woman in the world and was created from the skin of a dog.

◈ Car tyre shoes

Mexicans today are as inventive as they have always been in their use of craft materials. *Huaraches* are sandals that are worn all over Mexico. The soles are made of rubber from used car tyres! They are a good example of recycling materials and are very comfortable.

Jewellery and adornment

Anything worn to decorate the body can be considered jewellery. In ancient times jewellery was worn to show how important someone was or to symbolize their religious beliefs. Jewellery does not have to be made out of a precious material like diamonds or gold. In fact, all kinds of materials – shells, bones, feathers or even hair – can be made into jewellery.

Gold and silver

Before the Spanish invaded Mexico in 1519, gold was everywhere and the people were very skilful in making jewellery from it. The art of metalwork spread from the Andes mountains in South America north to Mexico. The **artisans** would melt the gold down and pour it into **intricate casts** to make impressive pieces of jewellery. Golden masks and chest ornaments were particularly popular. The Aztecs had an advanced knowledge of metalworking techniques and they organized themselves into separate guilds to create their work.

When the Spanish arrived, they were amazed not only at the amount of gold they found, but also at how little the native people valued it. The Aztecs prized the gold because it was the same colour as the Sun which they worshipped, not because it was a financially valuable metal.

A large amount of the silver mined every year comes from Mexico. In Taxco, in the state of Guerrero, hundreds of silversmiths make silver jewellery from this soft metal and sell it around the world. Silver earrings are particularly popular in Mexico, where babies' ears are often pierced soon after they are born. Silver crescent-shaped earrings called *arracadas* are typically Mexican. They are often **filigree**, which is fine silver wire that has been twisted into a delicate lacy pattern.

This jade ornament would probably have been worn by someone very important – a priest or a nobleman perhaps.

Today, when the *charros* (Mexican horsemen) dress up for a festival, they wear trousers with solid gold buttons down the sides, and belt buckles, stirrups, and spurs **inlaid** with silver.

Precious stones

Mexico is rich in minerals and precious stones. Turquoise, **obsidian**, onyx, amethyst and jade are plentiful. In Chiapas, pieces of amber – a fossilized **resin** often containing insects – are tied on cords around children's necks to protect them.

The Maya valued jade more highly than gold and made **pendants**, bracelets and masks from this green gemstone. They valued it so much that when a person died, a jade bead was placed in their mouth – in addition to other items that they would find useful in the **afterlife**. The Aztecs did this too.

Featherwork

In the Aztec region of Anahuac, feather workers commanded as much respect as goldsmiths. They lived in a special quarter of the city and made capes, shields and headdresses for the noblemen. They attached the feathers using paste and a needle and thread. Today, the dancers who perform *La Danza de los Concheros* during festivals carry feathered shields and wear feathered headdresses just as their ancestors once did.

Other materials

In Taxco, in the state of Guerrero, jewellers make beautiful pieces of jewellery out of abalone shell, which is valued for its **iridescent** colour. Cow horn, and tortoiseshell from the hawksbill turtle are used to make elaborate hair combs, carved in the shape of horses, crocodiles or mermaids.

Montezuma's headdress

When Hernán Cortés, the Spanish explorer, arrived in Mexico in 1519, the Aztec emperor Montezuma presented him with a magnificent headdress, as they thought he was a god. The headdress was made out of long green feathers, jade and gold beads. The brilliantly coloured feathers were from the quetzal, a sacred bird for the Aztecs.

During festival time, Mexican people dress up in traditional costumes such as this elaborate headdress - which is probably similar to the one worn by Montezuma, the Aztec emperor.

Displaying your beliefs

People choose to decorate their body for all sorts of reasons. What jewellery they choose to wear and how they wear it can tell us a lot about their beliefs and the culture they come from.

The **Huichol** are one of Mexico's **indigenous** people who live in one of the remotest parts of the country. They are a very religious group and show their beliefs through the clothes and jewellery they wear. They are very fond of glass beads and like to wear them as necklaces, or threaded on a net as a hat-band, belt or a shoulder-bag. The beads are arranged in patterns which are very symbolic to the group. For example, they believe the pattern of an eagle will guard the growing maize crop, and a zig-zag pattern symbolizes the rain.

The **Otomí** people also believe the things they wear will protect them. They hang tiny beaded sachets of herbs around their necks to protect them from diseases.

Jewellery instead of money

After the Spanish brought them to Mexico, glass beads were sometimes used to buy things instead of gold and silver. Today, glass beads are still valuable as **heirlooms** and are handed down from mother to daughter. In Najá you can see young girls weighed down with as many glass bead necklaces as they can possibly wear.

In the **Zapotec** area of the Oaxaca valley, the jewellery the women wear is very valuable. Instead of investing their money in the bank, the women prefer to invest it in their earrings and necklaces. During festivals, the women like to wear all their savings. Chokers, bracelets, earrings and heavy coin necklaces dipped in gold or silver are proudly worn to show how wealthy they are.

The Huichol group that lives in Jalisco is famous for patterned glass beadwork. Huichol beadwork is considered a high form of craftsmanship and requires great skill. In this design there are hundreds of tiny beads.

Throughout Mexico, silver coin necklaces and *milagros* make popular pieces of jewellery for people to buy.

Jewellery and religion

In the Yucatán the women wear long golden **rosaries** and golden filigree crosses during festivals to display their faith. Jewellers are often asked to make *milagros*, which means miracles in Spanish. People offer them to their favourite patron saint when they are hoping for a cure or as a thank you if their prayers have been answered. They ask the jeweller to make them something in the shape of the part of the body that is to be cured – like a leg, an arm or an eye. *Milagros* can be made out of gold, silver, tin, wood, or even bone and wax. They are either worn as a piece of jewellery or are attached to statues of the saints or to the walls of churches.

◇ Body art

The Maya practised tattooing – they painted intricate patterns on their bodies for spiritual reasons. A tattoo is a permanent design that is made on the body by piercing the skin and putting ink inside. Because having a tattoo was very painful, it was seen as a sign of bravery and courage. The Maya practised all sorts of body art – full body tattoos, facial tattoos, scarifications and piercings. The colours were very symbolic. Warriors were tattooed in red and black, young men were painted black until they married, priests and those who were about to be sacrificed were tattooed in blue, and prisoners were given black and white stripes.

Lacquering

When a wooden object is **lacquered**, it is given a shiny hard coat so that it is possible to eat or drink from it. In Mexico, all sorts of things are lacquered – trays, boxes, dishes and trunks are all lavishly decorated. Creating the shiny coat takes a very long time, often up to several days. A special paste is painted on, and when this has dried, it is polished with a soft cloth before another layer of paste is added. The wood that is used can be scented, and sometimes part of the wood is left bare to allow the fragrance of the wood to come through. Some of the most popular objects to be lacquered are gourds. These are made from natural fruits or vegetables, which can be made into bowls or cups to eat and drink from. Because lacquering takes such a long time, in some areas of Mexico gloss paint is being used nowadays instead.

There are generally two types of lacquer decoration commonly found in Mexico today – *rayada* (which is engraved), and *dorada* or *pincel* (which is painted).

The *rayada* technique

Powdered grey soil is added to the base black lacquer and the artist uses a special tool made out of a thorn to scratch out the design. The thorn is taken from a local thorn tree and inserted into a feather. The scratching reveals the black layer underneath and many **intricate** patterns are made by the artist. When the desired design has been achieved, the piece is then ready to be painted in bright colours.

The *pincel* technique

This involves painting intricate designs over the black lacquer layer. Each artist has their own technique, but often the painted design is raised slightly above the black layer to give a nice texture. The paint is applied using a *pincel*. The artist makes their own *pincel* from cat hairs which have been tied together and inserted into a feather. Because the cat hairs are so fine, the artist can paint very intricate designs. The coloured paints are made from powdered pigments. Different colours are added to white powder and a natural oil is added to make a thick paste.

◈ A long process

Before the lacquer is applied, the surface has to be sanded down so that it is perfectly clean and smooth. The lacquer is made from minerals and oils. A black powder called the *tizate* is made by grinding and baking the minerals calcium carbonate and magnesium. The *tizate* is then mixed with natural oils – it is this process which makes the lacquer hard and waterproof.

The oils are obtained from plants, seeds and insects. The gathering of the oils is a highly specialized task and requires detailed knowledge of the local natural resources. The quality of the *tizate* and oils is very important to the end appearance of the lacquer. The piece is then ready to be decorated.

Gourds

Gourds have been used in Mexico since ancient times. A gourd is made from a large fruit or vegetable such as a marrow or a pumpkin. The gourds are cut down from the tree and left to dry in the sun. When the gourd is hard and dry, it is cut down the middle and left in water until the insides rot. The flesh of the gourd is then soft enough to be scooped out. Because the gourd has been left to harden first before its flesh is scooped out, it keeps its shape. Once the gourd has been hollowed out, it is then ready to be decorated. One of the most popular methods is lacquering.

Gourds are used for all sorts of things. Traditionally they are used to drink out of, and in some parts of Mexico people still drink a hot drink called *atole* from gourds. *Atole* is a corn-meal gruel which is drunk with chilli pepper usually as the first meal of the day. Apparently drinking *atole* from a gourd makes it taste much nicer than drinking it out of plastic. In the North of Mexico gourds are used as bottles with a maize cob for a stopper. In the more rural areas, the rind of the fruit from the calabash tree makes good bowls from which to eat. They can also be used as strainers, made into musical instruments, handbags or even worn on the head to protect you from the sun.

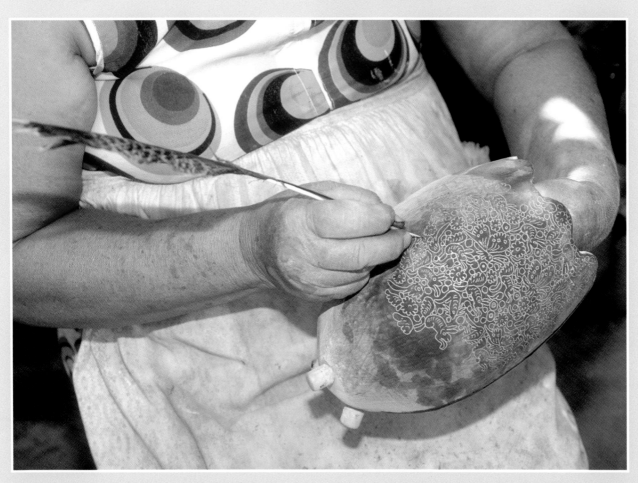

A special tool, made from a thorn inserted into a feather, is used to scratch an intricate design on the lacquer of this gourd before it is painted with bright colours and metallic dyes.

Masks

Masks have been worn in Mexico since ancient times. Some of the early Mexican peoples believed that everyone has two souls – one in the head and one in the heart. By covering your face with a mask they believed you would be able to get in touch with the spirit world. Today, masks are mainly used as a disguise to entertain audiences at festivals.

Regional dances, ceremonies and masks

Masks are usually worn for part of a festival or during a special dance. They are used to help tell a story, to entertain people, or to make fun of important people by making a **caricature** of them. They can be made out of all sorts of materials. The Maya made masks for their special ceremonies out of jade, which at the time was a very precious stone – even more valuable than gold.

The fair skin, blue eyes and facial hair of the European **conquistadors** fascinated the native peoples of Mexico, whose features were very different. These new faces inspired them to create masks showing their distinctive features. The masks were intended to make fun of the Spanish with their fine clothing, beards, fair skin and arrogant manner.

The artist Frida Kahlo can be seen holding a sad mask to her own face in this painting from 1945 called *The Mask*.

Masks in paintings

Masks remain very important in Mexican culture and often appear in the paintings of the 20th century artist, Frida Kahlo. Many of her **self-portraits** show her face as a mask under which she is hiding her true feelings. In *The Mask*, painted in 1945, this idea is reversed. Here a woman is holding a papier mâché mask up to her face. This time it is the mask that is showing her feelings as it is crying, and it hides her actual face.

Masks and dancing

There are many festivals in Mexico and they vary from region to region. Each festival usually has its own particular dance, which often has a religious significance. The dancers often wear wooden masks that are beautifully decorated. The dancer has to take a vow to promise God and the saints that they will perform the dance for a certain number of years.

In San Pablo Apetatitlán, during Carnival time, the villagers dance the Dandies' Quadrille. Each dancer wears a wooden mask that has been painted with oil paints and then rubbed with a dead chicken to protect the surface of the mask and make it shiny. The masks have glass eyes, which are attached to a thread that opens and shuts them. Although wood is the most popular material for making masks, leather, clay, papier mâché, gourds and wax are also used.

The Tiger Dance is a very old dance and dates back to ancient times. As there are no tigers in Mexico, these dances probably originally featured jaguars or ocelots. They show the tiger damaging the crops and being chased away by angry farmers. The tiger masks are made of wood and have real animals' teeth, hair and whiskers. They are often worn by children during the Day of the Dead festival.

Fiestas and festivals

Mexico is a country that takes its festivals very seriously. Some, like Independence Day, are celebrated throughout the country, whereas some are celebrated only in certain regions. At festival times, artisans make special objects for people to buy to decorate their homes and churches in celebration of these occasions. Mexico is a Roman Catholic country and much of the art that is created is connected with this religion.

Religion and art

On 12th December Mexicans celebrate the feast of the Virgin of Guadalupe, who is the patron saint of Mexico. The day celebrates the story of how the Virgin Mary appeared to a poor boy called Juan Diego. On this day, many people make a **pilgrimage** to the Virgin's shrine. The children dress up in traditional Native American dress and visit their churches. Little girls wear colourful necklaces, embroidered blouses and patterned shawls, and the boys wear serapes, sandals and painted moustaches. They are called *Dieguitos* after Juan Diego. On their backs the children carry little wooden frames from which hang all sorts of Mexican crafts such as tiny clay pots and **gourds**. The Virgin of Guadalupe is an extremely popular **icon** that has inspired a great deal of art, and many artists make painted sculptures of her.

At Christmas some regions stage *las posadas*. The word in Spanish means inns or shelters. Usually, on Christmas Eve people will take to the streets and re-enact the journey made by Mary and Joseph to Bethlehem. Sometimes people dress up as the couple, but often children carry candles and elaborately carved wooden figures of Mary and Joseph on a donkey. The parties go from door to door asking for people to give them shelter. Often they are refused, until finally one house

The Virgin of Guadalupe is a very inspiring image for many Mexican artists. Pictures, statues and ornaments are all created in her honour. People take images of the Virgin to be blessed after Mass.

Cinco de Mayo is an important day in the Mexican calendar. People dress up in traditional costumes and take to the streets in celebration, across Mexico and in Mexican communities in other countries. This parade is in New York City.

welcomes them in and they will be given Mexican chocolate and Christmas Eve *tamales* – which are corn husks, chillis and tomatoes. The end of the festival is when the children are allowed to break the **piñata**, a papier mâché toy that has been filled with toys and sweets.

Independence and revolution

September 16th is the day Mexicans celebrate their independence from Spain. Papier mâché helmets and trumpets are made in red, white and green – the colours of the Mexican flag. *Rehiletes* are sold, which are rather like feathered shuttlecocks on long sticks, painted in the national colours. Traditional food and drink is served. Every **plaza** in every town is covered with flags, balloons and strings of lights, and fireworks are lit.

Many Mexicans believe Independence Day should really be celebrated on the 5th May. *Cinco de Mayo* is the day they defeated the French army at the Battle of Puebla in 1862. Every year on this day the people of Mexico celebrate. There is **mariachi** music, traditional foods, bullfights, and colourful decorations. The women dress up as *soldaderas* – the women who travelled with the army to cook and care for the men. The men re-enact the battle between the French and the Mexicans, and at the end fireworks are let off to celebrate the Mexican victory.

Deaths and burials

In many parts of the world, death is something that is not spoken about a great deal. In Mexico, however, death is not such a forbidden subject, and family and friends who have died are remembered openly and their lives are frequently celebrated by those who miss them. Consequently, many of the arts and crafts in Mexico have to do with death. There are even children's toys that make fun of death.

El Día de los Muertos

El Día de los Muertos means 'The Day of the Dead' in Spanish. It is held every year on November 2nd. It is the most important festival in Mexico. On this day, people remember their relatives and friends who have died. They place lighted candles and flowers on their graves. Many Mexicans stay up all night to remember those who have died. Mexicans believe the dead come back to Earth on this day, and they cook the favourite food of the people who have died and place it on their grave or on household altars for them to eat. Many of the items that are made to celebrate The Day of

the Dead have a lot of humour in them and are designed to make people laugh. Throughout the year in Mexico, toymakers spend their time making the things they are going to sell for the Day of the Dead. These are enjoyed as much by the adults as by the children.

◈ Drawing the dead

An important part of the Day of the Dead celebrations is the acceptance and mockery of death. This is shown by the *calavera* or skeletons which can be seen everywhere during the festival in all sorts of funny poses. They were inspired by José Guadalupe Posada, a 19th-century Mexican artist and political cartoonist. He liked to draw skulls and skeletons to show how short life is and to make death seem less serious to the living. In his drawings he showed that whether you were a peasant or a politician, in death we are all the same. His drawings were often of poor people and their suffering and were always in black and white.

Skulls and skeletons

As November approaches, all the shops begin to fill up with toy coffins, cardboard skeletons whose legs move when strings are pulled, wooden roundabouts with little skeletons on horses, and clay skulls with moveable lower jaws. The windows of bread shops are painted with dancing skeletons, and inside they sell *panes de muertos*, which means the 'Bread of the Dead'. These are little figures made from bread dough which are sold all over Mexico. In Toluca they make skulls out of coloured sugar, and marzipan guitars filled with aniseed liquid as gifts for the living and for the dead. In Oaxaca they make tiny clay skeletons of wedding couples, priests hearing confessions, footballers and policemen.

The Day of the Dead festival inspires Mexicans to create skulls and skeletons from a wide range of unusual materials.

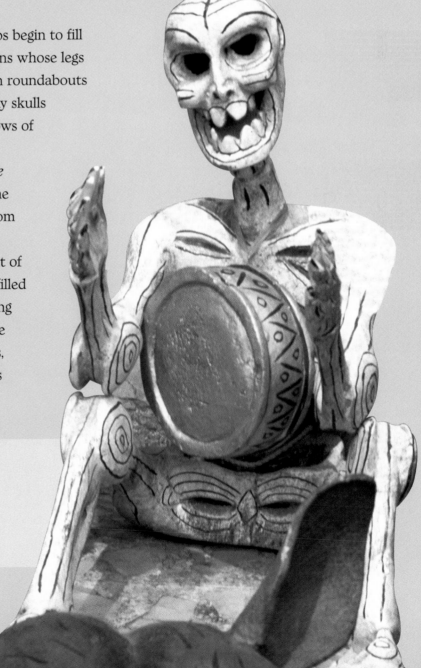

Painting

Painting in Mexico has a long history, and the earliest important examples date from the time of the Maya. At Bonampak in southern Mexico, several buildings are decorated on the inside with brightly painted murals. These murals, which were painted as **frescos**, provide important information about the everyday life of the Maya. Some include scenes of dancers and musicians, others show battle and torture. In most of the murals, the drawings are outlined in black and then filled in with brightly coloured pigments.

Other important examples of Mexican painting come from the city of Teotihuacan, where temples, homes, and other buildings were covered in murals. Although many of these paintings had to do with religion, they give important information about the social organization of the society. The relative sizes of people and objects, as well as what they are wearing, give clues about their importance.

◇ Mystery of the Mayan Blue

The colours used in the murals at Bonampak are particularly interesting, and archaeologists have been able to work out how they created the colours – all except one. The red and pink **pigments** were created from red iron oxide; the yellow, from hydrous iron oxide; the black from carbon; and the blue – though we know it is made from clay and indigo, no one is quite sure *how* it was made.

The murals at Bonampak are very important as they show in great detail how the Maya lived - the clothes they wore, the battles they fought, and the customs they carried out.

36

New rulers, new styles

After the conquest of Mexico by the Spaniards in 1521, Mexican painting changed dramatically. There were two main reasons for this. Firstly, the Spaniards came from a rich tradition of painting in Europe, where the **Renaissance** was changing the way that artists looked at their subjects. Secondly, the Spaniards brought their Roman Catholic beliefs to Mexico, and so much of the art produced after their arrival was concerned with Catholic themes.

During the first years after the Spanish conquest, some of the most important artists working in Mexico were actually foreigners. These artists, such as Baltazar de Echave and Andrés de la Concha, brought European techniques and subjects to Mexico. However, the Spanish also made use of the talents of native artists, often retraining them in Renaissance techniques. The work of these artists can be seen in hundreds of churches and monastries built by the Spanish.

An original genre

While most Mexican art at this time was heavily influenced by Spanish traditions, one original genre did develop – the caste painting. During the colonial period there was intermarriage between Mexicans and the Spanish administrators. The caste paintings, which were often taken back to Spain as souvenirs, claimed to show what the offspring of various racial mixes would look like. They each show a mother and father of different races with their child. These paintings were meant to be insulting, and are an example of the racist attitudes of the Spanish towards their Mexican subjects. However, the caste paintings are important because they are some of the only pieces of art from that period that show Mexicans from all walks of life.

Diego Rivera liked to paint people carrying out traditional Mexican skills as in *La Molendara* (The Grinder), depicting a woman rolling out tortillas.

Independence

For several decades after Mexico gained its independence in 1821, painting continued to follow European styles. It was not until the late nineteenth century that Mexican painting really began to develop its own features. Artists such as José Mariá Obregón began to mix **indigenous** and European subject matter. Also during this time, José Mariá Velasco was painting his unique landscapes. Then, after the turn of the twentieth century, Mexican painting came onto the world stage, thanks to two artists: Diego Rivera and Frida Kahlo.

Similar ideas, different approaches

Diego Rivera travelled to Europe at the age of 21 to study the works of the Great Masters. When he saw the Renaissance frescos in Italy, he knew that he had found his style. Rivera believed passionately in the rights of the working classes and did not like the idea of making paintings that would hang in galleries or the homes of the wealthy – he wanted everyone to be able to see his work. He began painting murals on the walls of public buildings, where ordinary passers-by would see them. His favourite subjects were scenes of ordinary Mexicans doing traditional things such as making tortillas (see picture on page 37) or grinding corn. He also painted many scenes of the Aztecs and the revolution against the Spanish.

Frida Kahlo shared her husband's love of Mexico and its traditions, as well as many of his political views. However, she developed her own unique artistic style. Kahlo had a difficult life – a bus accident as a teenager left her in constant pain, and her relationship with Rivera was often stormy – and her paintings reflect this. Like her husband, she used many images from traditional Mexican folk art, but her paintings often had a darker tone. She painted many self-portraits, often using masks or showing her poised between two different worlds (see page 30).

This fresco is called *People's Army* by David Alfaro Siquieros. It is a powerful image of the Mexican people preparing to fight the United States to reclaim the land that had been taken from them.

The Cemetery by José Clemente Orozco was painted in 1931. He was a very political artist whose work was always concerned with the plight of the Mexican people. When he was a child he met the renowned painter José Guadalupe Posadas who inspired him to become an artist.

A rich tradition

It was not just Rivera and Kahlo who were helping to make Mexican art popular throughout the world. Many other artists were exploring similar themes and styles. Several of them were influenced by the work of José Guadalupe Posada, who died in 1913.

Like Rivera, many Mexican painters of the early twentieth century were muralists. Their work was sometimes very political, which upset the government. These painters protested againt the government and went on marches to campaign for the ideas they believed in. They hoped that by painting on walls their message would reach as many people as possible, who would then want to join their cause. Some of these painters, like David Alfaro Siquieros, were sent to prison because of their beliefs.

José Clemente Orozco was a muralist who painted huge frescos showing the poor people of Mexico struggling to survive as they went about their everyday lives. His later work became influenced by **Expressionism** – he used fewer colours and relied on light to show the emotion in the painting.

Another artist, Rufino Tamayo, often painted Mexican people engaging in traditional activities. His paintings are a mixture of pre-hispanic Mexican art and more modern art from Europe. He was heavily influenced by **Cubism**, especially the works of the Spanish artist, Pablo Picasso.

Toys

Toys are very important in Mexico. There are some cities, such as Santa Cruz de las Huertas or Jalisco, which are famous because of the toys they produce. Originally the word toy described not just a child's plaything, but also anything that was small and collectable. In Mexico, many adults like to collect these miniature ornaments which are often very similar to toys. Although Mexican children today play with the same types of toys as children around the world, simple handmade toys are still very popular. The craft of making them is handed down from generation to generation. All sorts of things are used to create unusual toys. Simple natural materials that can be found locally like paper, wood, leaves, clay and tin are used rather than man-made plastics.

Puppets, dolls and pottery animals

Making and selling toys can be a way to earn a living in Mexico, just as it is anywhere else. Some children are taught from a very young age how to work with clay so they can make toys and earn money for their families. Children as young as seven make carefully modelled pottery animals such as dragons, snakes, armadillos and peacocks. Puppets are also very popular in Mexico. In other parts of the world puppets are often used to tell fairy tales such as Hansel and Gretel. But in Mexico, puppets are used for more political purposes. There is a famous puppet called Vale Coyote who was a bad character and used to make fun of the dictator Porfirio Diaz during the Revolution.

Like the rest of the world, dolls are a favourite toy for Mexican children. They can be made out of all sorts of things from papier mâché to bits of rag. Some are brightly painted and others are dressed in traditional costumes.

Musical toys are widespread. Clay whistles in the shape of an animal, black pottery flutes and white striped clay trumpets are all popular toys, as well as guitars that are a miniature version of an adult's.

Festival toys

Special toys are made for certain festivals in Mexico. For the Feast of Corpus Christi, which takes place in June, people give each other a *mulita* or mule to celebrate the day. They can be made out of palm leaves, rushes, banana wood or even the dried husks of corn on the cob. Some are small enough to wear as a brooch, while others are large enough to carry a child. On this day lots of these toy mules are lined up for sale outside the cathedrals in Mexico, with their **panniers** filled with flowers and fruit. They are a reminder of the real mules that used to wait outside the churches for their owners.

Puppet theatre

There was a very famous puppet company created by Leandro Rosete Aranda in Mexico City. In 1900 his theatre had a cast of over 5000 puppets! Audiences would come from all over the country to see famous puppets dance to the music of a live orchestra. Today, the puppets are still made with clay heads, arms and feet, which are painted and decorated with brightly coloured feathers.

The bodies and heads of these puppets are made of clay, but other local materials such as grasses, straw and wood are used to decorate the puppets. As well as depicting traditional stories, puppets are often used to make fun of leading political figures. Because they are puppets and not live actors, the stories they tell can be a lot more daring.

Paper

Mexicans have always been very creative in their use of paper. The Aztecs developed their own style of picture writing, which consisted of a series of pictures describing a religious or historical event. They wrote these down on paper made out of bark or on deer skin. These writings are called **codices** and they tell us a great deal about the Aztecs. The codices often show the deeds of gods and rulers or tell stories of battles. Bark paper is still very popular in Mexico today – particularly with the tourists who like to buy a traditional painting as a souvenir. Unfortunately, this has led to a shortage of the bark needed to create the paper.

◈ Making bark paper

There are two types of tree that are used. The fig tree gives a dark paper and the mulberry tree a whitish paper. Women are responsible for making the paper. The bark is peeled off the tree, washed then boiled in a cauldron for several hours. The fibres are laid in lines on a board and beaten with a stone until they fuse together. The paper is left in the sun to dry. Mexicans still record the happenings of village life on bark paper in a style that is similar to that used on the ancient codices.

Amate bark paintings are handmade by the Otomi Indians using the same method that was used in the 13th century. Very colourful birds or animals are painted on the paper.

Specially trained scribes wrote the Aztec codices using natural dyes on animal skin, bark paper from the bark of a fig tree or on cotton. This example shows the Aztec gods Xipe Totec and Quetzalcoatl, the plumed serpent.

Cutting out paper

Cutting pictures out of paper is a favourite craft in some areas of Mexico. In the **Otomí** village San Pablito, Puebla, they still believe in spirits – just as the Aztecs did. They cut the Spirit of the Tomato and the Spirit of the Banana out of bark paper to encourage their crops to grow. These paper seed spirits are shown holding ripe fruit and vegetables. Sometimes they are 'brought to life' by a **shaman** blowing into their mouths or holding them over incense smoke.

In Puebla and Veracruz people cut brightly coloured tissue and metallic paper into **intricate** designs. A very sharp chisel, a hammer and a razor are used to mark and cut out the patterns. Then these lacy papercuts are hung around the town or used to decorate the outside of churches on special occasions.

Papier mâché

In Mexico, making things out of papier mâché is a very skilled art form. It was invented by the Chinese who also invented paper. By the end of the 10th century, paper was more popular in Spain than the **papyrus** that they were using before. As paper is quite a cheap material and easy to obtain, you can find papier mâché artists all over Mexico making all sorts of amazing objects.

In other parts of the world, plastic is often used to make toys, but in Mexico quite elaborate toys are still made out of papier mâché. Puppets, masks, dolls whose arms and legs move, and rattles for babies are all made out of paper.

◈ How is it made?

Papier mâché is made by sticking layers and layers of paper onto a frame, which is usually made from chicken wire. Sometimes balloons or clay pots are used to stick the paper on. When the paper has hardened, the balloon or pot can be broken leaving just the shell of the papier mâché. This all takes a lot of time and a lot of hard work, but the results are well worth it. When the papier mâché is hardened it is ready to be decorated.

These hand puppets, for sale in a market, are made from papier mâché. Giant papier mâché puppets called *mojigangas* are paraded down the streets during carnivals and festivals.

Toys and celebrations

All sorts of things are made out of papier mâché for children during religious celebrations. The week before Easter is an important time for Mexicans. During this Holy Week, paper workers in Mexico City and Celaya spend all their time making papier mâché Judas dolls (named after Judas Iscariot – the apostle who betrayed Jesus). These come in many shapes and sizes and are meant to look quite frightening. Some look like grinning devils painted red, or skeletons, and sometimes they are made to look like popular characters. Traditionally the Judas dolls would have fireworks attached to them and be set alight in the streets on Easter Saturday. The Day of the Dead is another popular time for papier mâché skeletons and skulls.

Piñatas

At Christmas time and on birthdays, children in Mexico enjoy a special treat. A **pinata** is a special container that is filled with toys, sweets, fruit and nuts and then covered in layers and layers of papier mâché. All sorts of shapes are made – stars, fish, flowers, small boats, and even Donald Duck and Batman can all be made from papier mâché. At the end of the feast the *piñata* is hung up and the children are blindfolded, spun around and given a stick to try and smash the *piñata*. When the *piñata* breaks, all the children scrabble for the sweets and toys. The custom began about 500 years ago in Italy. At parties the host would fill fragile, pineapple-shaped pots (called *pignatte*) with treats for their guests. *Piñata* parties soon became popular in Spain, and the custom was brought to Mexico by the Spanish settlers.

Breaking the *piñata* is a special treat that all Mexican children look forward to.

Music and musical instruments

Mexico is a country full of music. Wherever you go, you will find musicians on street corners, in bars and restaurants and in people's homes singing traditional folk ballads and making music. This is particularly the case during festival times when bands and orchestras tour the streets dressed in traditional costumes. Mexicans also like to make their own musical instruments, and different regions of Mexico are famous for producing certain instruments.

Instruments from different regions

In the Sierra Madre mountains of Mexico there is a town called Paracho, which is known as the guitar capital of Mexico. Everybody who lives in the town is involved in some way with the building of guitars. People come from all over the world to hear and buy these guitars, as the sound that they produce is so good. The reason they are unique is that, unlike many guitars, the ones from Paracho are made by hand. A variety of simple tools are used to cut and plane the wood, the most useful being the *cuchillo*, a type of sharp knife used by all the guitar makers to cut the wood. Different types of wood are used on the front, back and sides of the guitar, each one creating a different sound. One of the most popular woods is Mexican rosewood.

Veracruz is famous for its harps and harp music. Like the guitar, the harp is a very popular instrument during festivals – particularly the religious ones. The *arpa veracruzana* is the folk harp made in this area. It has between 32 and 36 strings which are made from animal gut, and the harp measures up to 1.5 metres high.

In the town of Paracho the art of making guitars by hand is a tradition that is passed on to each generation.

Strolling bands

The folk harp is usually played with other stringed instruments by the strolling musicians who move from table to table in bars and restaurants singing songs for the customers. These groups are called **mariachi** and they usually consist of two violins, two five-string guitars, and a guittarón, which is a large bass guitar, and often a pair of trumpets. All the musicians are expected to sing and often they improvize or make up the songs to suit their customers, charging their customers for each song they sing. Mariachis can be found all over Mexico, but they originate from Jalisco. They are easy to spot by the traditional costumes they wear – the wide-brimmed Mexican hat and a tight-fitting suit with silver buttons down the front.

The flamboyant costumes worn by the Mariachi musicians and the vibrant music they play make it easy to spot these strolling players all over Mexico.

Cross-currents

In towns along the Mexico/US border the cross-currents of Mexican and US culture have led to many snack vendors selling food and drink from both countries.

In the north, Mexico borders the US states of California, Arizona, New Mexico and Texas. It is in these states in particular that we can see the influence that Mexican art has had on US art.

Mixing cultures

Some people who live near the US border travel to the United States to work, and return home again in the evening. They are known as migrant workers. This mixing of the cultures has meant that Mexican art has become popular with many people in the USA. Papier mâché and silver jewellery are particularly popular. Tijuana in the north of Mexico is a very popular holiday destination for many Americans and a lot of

silversmiths work in this town. Tourism has led to an increase in the popularity of Mexican art in other countries too. Places like Cancún and Acapulco are places people like to go on holiday, and Mexican art makes great souvenirs.

The festival of Cinco de Mayo is probably more popular amongst Mexicans who live in the United States than it is in Mexico. This is perhaps because they are not living in their home country and feel more nostalgic about where they were born. At this time, people in the United States like to eat Mexican food and dress up in traditional Mexican clothing, and the children will break open a *piñata*.

Famous artists

The artists Frida Kahlo and her husband Diego Rivera have had a great influence on art in Europe and the rest of the world. They were both inspired by folk art and the art of the ancient civilizations, which they included in their paintings. When they became famous artists and their work became known around the world, Mexico and its history were introduced to people who until then probably knew very little about the Mexican way of life. Frida Kahlo was famous for wearing traditional Mexican dress and lots of **pre-Hispanic** jewellery. When her hand, wearing a Mexican ring on every finger, was seen in the fashion magazine *Vogue*, it started a trend amongst jewellery designers, who began to copy Mexican-style jewellery.

Tina Modotti was born in Italy in 1896, but she moved to Mexico and worked as a photographer. She became a Communist and her photographs are famous for their revolutionary images of working-class Mexicans and Mexican **artefacts** such as an ear of dried corn, a sickle, and a guitar.

Francisco Toledo is a **contemporary** artist who was born in Oaxaca in 1940. He worked in Paris for a while, but when he returned to Mexico he dedicated himself to the promotion of the traditional arts and crafts of his home state, Oaxaca. He expresses his art in many ways – in tapestries, pottery, sculpture, as well as in paintings. He is well known for not only being an exceptional artist, but also somebody who wants to protect the native traditions of Mexico.

In the 20th century, for the first time in history, Latin American art became famous around the world. Collectors and museums wanted to buy paintings by the Mexican artist Rufino Tamayo. His work was influenced by pre-Hispanic art as well as more modern European styles.

Today Frida Kahlo is as renowned as her husband Diego Rivera. Her dramatic life has provided fantastic material for a very successful Hollywood film about her life and work. Here, the actress Salma Hayek, herself an example of the success of Mexican artists and performers in the USA, waits on the set of the film.

◈ Mexican music

Traditional *mariachi* music has become commercialized in Europe and the United States. *La Bamba* was originally a traditional Mexican folk song with many improvized verses. It became an international hit in the 1980s and, although the tune is the same, it bears little resemblance to the original folk version.

Influence from abroad

For many years the native people of Mexico have been carrying on the traditions of their ancient ancestors and making art and crafts in the same way by hand. However, today it is becoming increasingly difficult for artisans to continue working in this way. The pace of life is changing in Mexico and more and more people are using machines to make things, as this is a lot less time-consuming and so they can make more profit when they sell their work.

Plastic and nylon

Where once people used natural materials that they found locally, today these are in many cases being replaced with artificial materials such as plastic – a material that can be easily moulded using machines. Many pots that used to be made out of clay are now made out of plastic. In many villages nylon dresses which are made by a machine are replacing the beautiful hand-woven *huipiles* with their embroidered designs. This is partly because women prefer to wear a more modern style of dress.

The **lacquering** of gourds is another example of a traditional craft that is dying out. Traditionally gourds are lacquered by hand and it takes many days to build up the layers of lacquer on the fruit. The effect is very beautiful, but it does take a long time. Sadly, more and more workers are using artificial gloss paints instead as this is much quicker and more profitable.

Using machines to make things instead of crafting something by hand means you can produce larger quantities in less time and so make more money. But the objects are not as individual as those that have been handcrafted.

This young boy and his grandfather illustrate the variety of clothing found in Mexico today. Both traditional and modern styles are widely-worn.

Television, advertising and films

Another reason why some of the ancient traditions are dying out is that children are reluctant to learn the skills from their parents. Television has meant that people see what is being done in other countries and they no longer find the more traditional way of life so appealing. This is leading to a decline in the popularity of the handmade toy market. Children who live in the cities know all about cars and computer games and are not interested in simple toys like pottery whistles that entertain village children. Today, the hand-crafted toys are largely made by elderly people, who make little profit. Their descendants are not likely to carry on the tradition.

Advertising is also responsible for the gradual disappearance of some traditional crafts. In many parts of Mexico, Father Christmas and Christmas trees – traditions which started in Europe – are now being adopted by many Mexicans and are replacing traditional customs such as the clay nativity scenes. The influence of the film industry has had a big effect on the things people like to buy, and characters such as Batman are more in demand than traditional cultural figures.

A richer culture

Throughout its history Mexico has been invaded by many countries. These different cultures have had a great influence on Mexican art. When the Spanish arrived, they brought with them particular methods of making things and special materials that could not be found in Mexico. The art of **filigree** became a popular craft in Mexico because it was very popular in Spain at that time. Before the conquest, craftspeople only used materials that were **indigenous**. Afterwards, they imported things such as wax and lead from other countries. They adopted new skills from other countries too, such as glass-blowing and making papier mâché.

The aim of most contemporary Mexican artists is to make pieces of art that have a strong Mexican flavour, but which include the styles of Spain, Native America and Europe as well. The art that is produced in Mexico is very rich and varied because of the many cultures that have gone into making the country what it is today.

51

Further resources

More books to read

Levy, Elizabeth, *Awesome Ancient Ancestors (America's Horrible Histories)* (Scholastic, 2001)

Baquedano, Elizabeth, *Eyewitness: Aztec, Inca & Maya* (Dorling Kindersley, 2000)

Nicholson, Robert, *Interfact: Aztecs* (Two-Can Publishing, 1998)

Parker, Edward, *Mexico* (Hodder, 2001)

Steele, Philip, *The Aztec News* (Walker Books, 2000)

Websites

http://www.aztecs.org.uk
A fascinating insight into the lives of the Aztecs which serves as a great backdrop to the exhibition at the Royal Acadamy of Arts, London

http://www.yahooligans.com/ arts_and_entertainment/Art/
Type in *Mexican* in the search box and have a look at a host of great sites

http://www.demon.co.uk/mexuk/meet_mex
A great introduction to the art and culture of Mexico

http://www.mexicanmuseum.org/
A lively website which explores the complexity of Mexican and Latin cultures in the Americas

http://www.nmwa.org/collection/profile.asp?LinkID= 471
A museum website dedicated to women in art with an interesting page on Frida Kahlo

http://www.diegorivera.com/index.html
A website dedicated to the work of Mexico's most celebrated muralist

Places to visit

UK
British Museum, London – especially the Department of Ethnography

Americas
The National Anthropology Museum, Mexico City

The Mexican Museum, San Francisco

Australia
The National Gallery of Australia, Canberra

Glossary

afterlife place where some people believe we go when we die

aqueduct bridge that carries water across a valley

archaeologist somebody who studies history by digging up and examining remains in the earth

artefact object that has been crafted

artisan craftsperson

axis an imaginary line that divides something exactly into two halves

basalt dark volcanic rock

bracket a support which is attached to, and sticks out from something which is vertical

candelabrum large candlestick with many branches for putting candles in

canvas coarse cloth that is used as a surface for oil-painting

caricature funny cartoon drawing of somebody that exaggerates their features

cast molten metal is poured into a mould to produce a certain shape

causeway a raised road or track above low ground or a stretch of water

characteristic feature or quality which is typical of something or somebody and distinguishes it from something or someone else

codex (plural **codices**) ancient picture writings of Mesoamerica

colonial styles and culture that came from Spain

conquistadors Spanish explorers who conquered the Aztecs and the Maya

contemporary anything which is up to date or modern

criollos white Mexicans who were descended from people in Europe

Cubism a movement in art in which objects are painted so that they look like they are made up of lots of angular shapes

exploited when somebody takes advantage of someone else who is usually weaker or less powerful than they are

Expressionism a movement in painting when the artist tries to paint the feelings of a person and not what they actually look like

feminist icon a famous woman who is admired by other women and inspires them

filigree technique which involves twisting fine gold or silver wire into delicate patterns

firing process in which clay is heated up to a very high temperature and turned into pottery

fresco painting on a wall or a ceiling, done whilst the plaster is still wet

glaze fix paint to pottery to create a shiny surface

gourd a fleshy fruit or vegetable with a hard skin that is dried and can be used to drink from

heirloom object – usually of value – that you inherit from your parents or relatives

Huichol traditional group who live in the Sierra Madre, a mountainous area in one of the remotest parts of Mexico. They are very cut off from the rest of the country and they still worship ancient gods.

icon an image that inspires worship

indigenous somebody who has been born in a country or region

inlaid when one material has been used to fill another so that both surfaces are flat

inscription words that have been written on an object such as an artwork

intricate quite complicated, detailed and delicate

iridescent giving off shiny rainbow-like colours

kerosene fuel made from paraffin oil

kiln oven used to heat clay and turn it into pottery

lacquer apply a substance which, when it dries, becomes a shiny, hard protective coat

Lancandón native group whose religious beliefs and practices have been inherited from the Maya

lintel a piece of timber that sits horizontally at the top of a door frame

Maiolica earthenware with coloured patterns on white enamel tin

maríachí popular Mexican strolling bands of musicians, which usually include two violins, two five-string guitars, a large bass guitar, and a pair of trumpets

mestizo people of mixed Spanish and Native American ancestry who make up about 60 per cent of the population of Mexico

migrate when people or animals move from one area to live in another

Modernist a movement in art which expresses modern ideas and designs

motif distinctive feature or ornament that is easily identified

mural decoration painted or carved on a wall

Native Americans the peoples and their descendants who lived in the Americas before the Europeans arrived

nomadic referring to a group of people who have no fixed place to live. They spend their lives moving from one place to another.

obsidian dark, glassy volcanic rock which is extremely hard

opaque cloudy and you cannot see through

ornate with a lot of decoration

Otomí traditional group who live chiefly in the State of Mexico and in central Hidalgo. Most of the people are Catholic although some in the village of San Pablito still honour the ancient gods.

pannier a basket, usually one of a pair, that can be carried on the back of a mule

papyrus a type of paper that is made from the stems of a plant of the same name that grows in water

pendant a jewel that hangs on the end of a necklace

peninsula a piece of land that sticks out into a sea or lake, so that it is almost completely surrounded by water

pigment part of a dye which colours something

pilgrimage religious journey to a certain sacred place

piñata treat for children during festivals. Sweets and toys are hidden in a clay pot that has been decorated with papier mâché. The children are blindfolded and then try and break the pot with a stick to release the sweets and toys.

plaza central open square in a city

poncho simple garment like a blanket with a slit in the top for the head

post-Conquest a word that describes anything which existed after the Spanish conquered Mexico

pre-Hispanic anything which existed before the Spanish arrived in the Americas

profit amount of money you make when you sell something after you have deducted what it cost you to buy

raze to destroy or tear something down

renaissance used to describe anything in art that is a new way of doing something. It is particularly associated with Italy in the 14th –16th centuries when people began to think about art in a new way.

renowned well known or famous

resin a sticky substance which comes from trees such as fir or pine

ritual act performed in a certain prescribed order

rosary string of beads which Roman Catholics use to keep count of the number of prayers they have said to God

rubble broken bits of stone used to fill in a hole before cement is added

self-portrait picture of yourself

shaman person who is thought to be in touch with the spirit world

sisal Mexican plant with large leaves that can be used to make ropes

solstice the times when the sun is furthest from the equator. These occur once in the winter – the Winter Solstice, and once in the summer – the Summer Solstice.

sophisticated something or somebody which is quite complicated and highly developed

spindle small bar that can be used by hand to wind and twist thread

summit the highest point

symmetrical exactly the same on opposite sides

synthetic something that has not been made out of natural materials but out of man-made ones

talisman object that people think has special magic power and will bring the owner good luck

tension when something like a piece of wool is stretched from one point to another so that it doesn't go slack

tortilla thin, round flat cake made from maize or corn meal and baked on a flat stone. It can be eaten with meat, chillies or beans.

warp threads which are stretched lengthways in a loom across the weft

weft threads that go sideways in a loom across the warp

Western hemsiphere the half of the earth containing the Americas

Zapotec traditional group that lives in Oaxaca. Their language is divided into many dialects. They make very fine pots, and serapes made on treadle-looms. The women are famous for their extravagant clothing.

Index